Yashodhara

Six Seasons Without You

Published in Sydney by Wild Peony Pty Ltd ABN 52 002 714 276
PO Box 636 Broadway NSW 2007 Australia
Fax: 61 2 9267 0688

International Distribution:
University of Hawaii Press
2480 Kolowalu Street
Honolulu, Hawaii 96822, USA
Fax: 1 808 988-6052

Asian Studies Book Services
Franseweg 55B
3921 DE Elst
Utrecht
The Netherlands
Fax: 00 31 318 470 073
E-mail: info@asianstudiesbooks.com
Web: http://www.asianstudiesbooks.com

First Published 2003

ISBN 1 876957 05 0

Printed in Australia by Southwood Press Pty Ltd, Marrickville, NSW.

Yashodhara

Six Seasons Without You

Subhash Jaireth

Wild Peony

Poetry 4

Acknowledgments

I am grateful to Judith Beveridge, Suzanne Falkiner, Alan Gould, Coral Hull, Nick Jose, Geoff Page and Judith Rodriguez for their support.

I also thank the Art Gallery of New South Wales for permission to reprint the following watercolour from its collection:

The month of Bhadon
INDIA Rajasthan Bundi, c 1675
opaque watercolour with gold on paper, 25.3 x 16.3cm (image)
Margaret Hannah Olley Art Trust 1991
Art Gallery of New South Wales
photograph: Ray Woodbury for AGNSW

For HJ, KJ and MJ

A Few Words to Begin With

This is the story of Yashodhara also known as Gopa or Bimba, the wife of Sidhartha, also known as Gautama, the would-be Buddha. The legends tell us that Gautama, the Sakya prince, was born in the 6th century BC near the present day Lumbini in south-western Nepal. His father was the king of a small warrior tribe of the Sakyas based in the principality of Kapilavastu. His mother Mayadevi died seven days after giving birth, and Gautama was brought up by his aunt, the younger sister of his mother. When Gautama was twenty-nine he left his palace, and his wife and new-born son Rahul to search for love, peace and salvation. Ananda, his cousin, spent more than twenty-five years looking after the Buddha. The Buddha died at a place called Kushinagar, not far from Kapilavastu. He was eighty-seven.

In telling the story of Yashodhara I have chosen a poetic form that was popular in ancient and medieval Indian, Sanskrit and non-Sanskrit literatures. The most famous work of the genre is the romantic poem *Ritusamharam*, The Gathering of Seasons, composed by Kalidasa, a fifth-century poet and dramatist. In Indian literatures one can also find a poetic form known as *Barahmasa*, twelve months, where each of the twelve months is described in a rhymed quatrain. The most famous of these, the *Gita-Govinda*, was written by the twelfth-century Bengali court poet Jayadeva. Some of these works inspired the sixteenth-century Indian miniature paintings of the *Ragamala* series that visually explore the relation between ragas and time or seasons.

My story of Yashodhara employs two voices. The season-poems are written in the voice of Yashodhara and follow a strict poetic structure. The relatively long narrative poems, which interject the season-poems, are written in the voice of a contemporary narrator. I feel that this voice helps me to interrogate the mythical nature of the Buddha's story. The aim was not only to re-tell the major events of the Buddha's story but also reveal the ways these stories were possibly made and told.

In telling these stories about Yashodhara and the Buddha I have used material from the following books: Jean Boisslier, *The Wisdom of the Buddha* (London: Thames and Hudson, 1994); Roberto Calaso, *Ka* (London: Vintage, 1999); Sherab Chodzin Kohn, *The Awakened One: A Life of the Buddha* (London: Phoenix, 1994).

Death of the Buddha

The word had spread
that in the last watch of the night
the Buddha would be extinguished without residue.
The flame would depart.
The Tathagatha, he, who-came-thus,
would be gone, never to come back.

Thus, that's the word
with which the story has to begin.
A word without meaning of its own.
A word nothing but a join, a stitch,
a recess, a pause to take a breath,
to listen to the silence before uttering the next word,
to make place for, to be ready to make place for.

To begin at the end,
where every beginning begins.

Before the bird flies,
in the mind
the flight has already taken place,
the wings have felt the twitch,
the air is full of expectation,
the trees stand with eyes wide open,
and the leaves smile.

The world is ready
for the story to unravel.

That year
the rains were late,
but when they came
there was no end to the inundation.
The rivers were overflowing
and the sky was moist,
dripping and succulent.

It was then
that the Buddha decided
that the time had come
to walk back to the place
where it had all started.

He was old and sick,
and the body,
afflicted by niggling pain,
was losing its grit.
The joy of talking
and listening to the people had faded
like the colour of his saffron robe.
Only walking
and the sound of footsteps
kept the pain at bay.

"I'm an old cart, held together
in vain by thin belts,"

he whispered to Ananda,
as they approached the sala woods near Kushingar,
just a smell away from Lumbini,
the final destination.

Like the dying Buddha
painted on the wall of a dark cave in south India,
I see him lying on his right side.
His head pointing to the north,
feet slightly bent like the spine of a question mark.
His left hand stretched along his body
as if it were the branch of a fallen tree.
The chest nothing
but a wrinkled parchment of a dry leaf.
The face, under the shadow of two blissfully flowering trees,
looking west, sad
but glowing like the late evening sun of the fading day.

He was dying,
but why this desire to go back
to the dusty streets of his childhood?
Why this urge to re-treat, re-trace and re-track
the forgotten face of memory.

The Freudian in me
will readily find
lurking behind
the grey shadows of guilt,
the search for a lost mother
hidden behind the figure of her sister

or was it the sight of the sad black magnificent eyes
etched like two little windows on the beautiful face of Yashodhara?

A body so immaculate, so luscious,
a soul so gentle and forgiving.

But did she really forgive him
for the years lost and betrayed?
Was he really
looking for forgiveness,
he, the blessed-one,
who knew the power of forgiveness?
Didn't he know
that she had died some thirty years ago,
praying to join the sangha,
shave her long black hair
and become invisible
behind the saffron robe of a bhikkhuni?

We leave, like footprints,
the shadows of desire, guilt, shame and kindness
in places whose dust sticks to us
and walks with us all our lives,
like ghosts, nagging us to re-turn and re-trieve.

Thus, he,
on his way back to the place of his birth,
was dying, as we all die,
lost, helpless and forlorn.

"Come and sit with me,"
he said to Ananda,
struggling to remember the final dream
seeping through the seams of his brain like a warm,
luminous, sweet and sonorous fog.
"I was", he whispered,
"king of the deer
and the forest had been set on fire by the musk hunters.
We knew
there was no one to help us,
and, as it always happens,
there was only one exit
through the thicket of trees
across a dangerous creek.

"I looked at them
and saw death in their eyes and knew
that they needed someone
to turn into a bridge.
One by one
they walked over me
leaving on me the footprints of their escape.

"There was one pretty fawn
who hesitated,
turned her head,
looked at me with her faultless eyes,
walked across gently
as if taking care not to hurt,
and sped away.

Who was
the pretty fawn, Ananda?
Did we ever…?"

And he died
before completing the question.
The lips quivered,
the mouth froze midway
holding onto the words
stuck like half-eaten seeds of a pomegranate.

He died as we all die,
with no Cross to carry
except his long life.
No betrayals, no atrocities, no resurrection,
a slow disappearance
into the last watch of the night.

The body washed and cleaned,
dressed in a fresh bright robe,
was placed on the sandalwood pyre
and set alight.
The wooden slippers
that hugged the feet
looked stranded,
misplaced and lonely beside the fire.
A horde of Brahmins fed and feasted.
The ash, divided into seven pitchers,
was given away to the seven mighty kings
who in time would erect seven stupas in their capitals.

I wonder
who received
the wooden slippers of the Buddha
the Tathagatha,
the one who-went-away-thus?

Summer 1

It's hot and there is no other word
to describe it, as day and night the wind blows

and dust masks the moon
that burns like the sun at noon, and the noon is like fire

unable to let the chandan paste
cool the skin. You ask me to cover my body

with wet lotus-leaves and stretch
like a sheet over you on the mat spread on the floor.

The maid swings the fan and coolness
spreads like streams to be replaced soon by flames.

The night passes leaving the sleep unslept
and brings day as if it were standing at the door

like an impatient guest,
unasked, unwanted, shameless and rude.

Summer 2

We shall cut two holes in the melon
and plunge our mouths in the dripping

white and red softness
textured by the crusty blackness of seeds

and suck, chew and spit
raising our heads to steal a glance at each other's insatiability

till our lips, teeth, and then tongue
meet to reach the warm softness of another kind

called a kiss and the journey will begin once again
which won't take us anywhere, but the promise will be there

so will be the temptation and desire.
And removing the green skin of the melon

dotted with white spots from over our heads,
we'll ask the summer and the heat to persist for a few more weeks.

Summer 3

The pond has dried
and cracks in the parched skin of the clayey bed

are dreaming the watery dreams
of fish, frogs, crabs, snakes, lotuses and lilies.

I put the hot crust to my mouth
and, hissing, the saliva disappears.

The clay is chewy, warm, sweet and sticky
and at night when you kiss me I hear you whisper of ripples

as my nipples grow hard and itchy,
I know a purple lotus — a baby elephant —

wants to grow in me. But this summer
it is hotter than ever and the pond inside me has dried:

no ripples, no splashes, an empty sky —
bland and stunned — and water turned into silence.

Summer 4

Once again
the drummers have come to play on their red pitchers

the sounds of yet-to-be-born clouds.
They sit in the copious shade of a large pepal,

their pitchers held tight between their legs.
As they play, their palms and fingers slide, beat and thump,

the neck, mouth, belly and hips of the round,
reddish vessels, and sounds fill me as if I too were a pitcher.

But you, my love, surely know
who is the real drummer that plays on me

and takes me to the distant snow-clad peaks
that I see from the window on dark, moonless nights.

Soon the drummers will stop, gather their pitchers
and depart, leaving behind the sounds of the thundering clouds.

Summer 5

Last night as I dipped
my hands in the pitcher

I found the moon
shimmering in the bowl of my cupped hands

and leaking through the fingers.
I drank the moon that night, but what's more

with the moon, I drank you.
He had, as you would have guessed, your face,

serene, sombre, silent,
but ready to smile. I walked on the warm, clayey roof

with that yet-to-appear smile
listening to the steps, and waiting for the red and yellow streak

to crack open the sky
announcing the dawn of a new hot summer's day.

Summer 6

Look Ma, look, little Rahul grabs my hand
and takes me to the window to show through the crack

the whirlwinds of dust
swooshing across the river bed.

Peacock feathers, slippers, shirts, banana leaves
and a poor black kitten churned up high and dropped,

to be lifted again, till they are all out of sight.
But they are not gone, the wild brigands,

and will return soon in greater numbers
to rattle the roofs, doors, windows, and Rahul

will hide his face holding me tight. Don't worry,
I'll whisper. It's nothing but wind rowdy, angry and fearsome,

as it should be, and it's having fun like you when you chase
with your friends the white pigeons cooing in the warm sunshine.

Four Encounters

I have been shocked
many times in my life
by the inhumanity of humans.

For instance:
the lunar landscape of Grozdnyi
and the face of a young boy
sitting beside the rubble
looking at the dead face of his mother;

the blindfolded Kurds
lined up against the wall
ready to be shot,
the blood about to escape
on the surface of the photo;

the Holocaust, Hiroshima,
the famine in Africa
and the killing fields of Rwanda, Cambodia…;

a man in a three-piece suit
hitting his wife
on a busy Sydney street;

a middle-aged woman
deliberately running over
her neighbour's dog;

Igor, the ten-year-old boy
from Chernobyl,
asking for his stump-like feet
a pair of soccer shoes;

and I can't forget,
among many other things,
the photo of Billy, Jenny and Little Toby
the three "veritable blood-thirsty beasts"
of Cunningham's circus,
shot by Prince Roland Bonaparte in Paris,
with his stuffed pet dog in the foreground.

I have been shocked
many times in my life
by the shock and by
the incredulity of our response:

a Guernica, a poem, a song,
a cheque of fifty or so dollars,
a letter of protest,
a tree planted in a memorial walkway.

A stop, a comma, a pause,
a necessary hiatus,
before we once again

ease into the normal
everyday flow of life.

So, what was the shock
that the young Gautama felt
when one fine summer morning
he asked Chandaka, his groom,
to saddle the white horse,
and to come with him for a trot
outside the walls of the palace garden?

He first saw
an old man,
then a sick man,
and finally a dead man.

The next day
he saw a sadhu with a bowl
begging for alms.

He was twenty-nine then
beaming with beauty, strength,
poise and confidence,

and the world was nothing
but a blank sheet of paper
waiting for him to leave
the hieroglyphs of his being and becoming.

"I was delicate, monks,"
he seemed to have said,
"extremely delicate, too delicate,"
like one of the lotuses
in his blue, red and white ponds.

Each time he was helped
into tunics, robes and cloaks
imported from miles-away Varanasi
he was bewitched
like a musk deer
at the immaculate shape
and the intransigence of his body.

Whose truth
had he come to believe in?
Was nature itself
tricking him
by showing only
the bright side of the pock-faced moon?

He encountered three men,
one after another,
followed by a fourth,
designed as if it were a nod, a gesture,
a finger pointing at the door
from where
the journey of disengagement had to begin.

I like this story
which nevertheless disturbs me
by being so neat in its structure and intent,
as if it were written by the hand of God,
as if it were, like most stories, composed post factum.
I am unsettled
by its self-assuredness,
its godly gaze,
its blatant constructed-ness.

Why is it
that a vase sculpted by a potter
doesn't unsettle me?
Why do I readily accept and enjoy
the wonderful sounds of a Bach cantata?
Is this because life,
be it of humans or gods, is awesome
due to its unharnessed messiness?

The night after the fourth encounter
Gautama,
the handsome prince of the Sakyas,
would leave his palace, wife and son,
to become the great renouncer.

The life of Gautama,
Yashodhara, Rahul,
and of many more people around him
would change for ever.

The Rains 1

For three days and nights
the clouds have come and gone without bringing a drop.

I have walked from house to house,
room to room, window to window, and felt you walk behind me

like a bewitched deer.
O when will you come, my love, and kiss my neck,

lift the soft, round bun of hair,
and whisper in my ear moist lusty groans?

It's silly of me but I wait for you
to paint the yellow sticky mud on my body

and summon four white elephants,
their trunks heavy with water smelling of lotuses and lilies,

to roar, tumble and rain like four
lover-clouds, each of them you, and yet different.

The Rains 2

Two elephants are playing
in the pond and two dark clouds in the sky.

Between the pond and the sky
I, like the moist air, thick, heavy, languid and translucent.

Two elephants are playing in my body
one you and the other the insatiable desire.

The first jumps out of the pond and raising
her trunk rains showers on the muddied wrinkles of the other,

after which they change places,
the showered and the showerer, the lover and the loved.

Two elephants are dreaming
in my dream and the rain falls in my sleep and outside.

The night is wet and my bed empty
waiting in vain for you to come and rain.

The Rains 3

No this is not the rain I am waiting for
but the one that wets my every inner fold.

Don't hold me like this
when you aren't with me but, sitting under some shady fig,

are lost in the realm of the thoughtless-ness.
The kheer in the golden bowl which Sujata, the young girl,

would one morning bring, would be sweet,
because the water with which it would be cooked would be me.

You have, I know, renounced me and the world
in order to listen to the celestial rain that showers

on the landscape of your thoughts,
but the foolish thought which warms my heart

tells me that it is me, your Gopa, who flows in you,
and like the rain feeds your body, thought and soul.

The Rains 4

It would be me;
you don’t know it yet, but it would certainly be me,

the rain drop
that would one day suddenly fall into your open mouth,

my white, limy and silky mollusc
and turn your blind thought into a pearl with which

you would bewitch a swarm of words,
to keep us enthralled, amazed and in awe.

The unblemished water
you would bring to us would quench our thirst,

because it would be you
who would have also brought the thirst. O, my love,

my deep and cool well, I am the brown grainy sand
that fills you, and turns your water sweet and fragrant.

The Rains 5

The rain has stopped
and the sun looking through the clouds enters my body,

moist and hot, like you, my elephant man, my lover.
Don't make love to me when it rains, I ask you often,

although you know that when it rains
I always wait for you to come, grab me and lift my sari and

from the back enter like a cloud.
And in the evening when I go out looking for little Rahul,

my friends enchanted by my
elephant-like walk and the chime of silver anklets stop

and ask me: O look how you glow!
Tell us please what has taken you over? In reply

I smile and they know that the cloud-elephant
which carried water from the honey-filling seas has emptied into me.

The Rains 6

I come out on the roof
to hear the rain at night and to watch the wet moon,

but the moon has absconded,
and the sky, loaded with dark, heavy clouds,

splinters into flashes of crimson and yellow
and bursts like a pomegranate.

I hear thunder roll through the sky like a herd
of baby elephants trumpeting through the fields of sugarcane,

when the fire starts, first as a spark,
then flares up reaching the canopy of wet leafy trees,

and suddenly the shower begins.
Drops like warm, crusty walnuts hit my body stretched on the floor.

What's that, I ask myself, which makes
the ache and the grief so sensuous and pleasing?

The Departure

Thus one summer night,
in the lunar month of Ashadha
when the moon was full
and the harsingar bloomed to perfection,
Gautama stepped out of the palace.

A night earlier
Yashodhara had woken up
disturbed by a nightmare,
wet with sweat and short of breath.
"A mad elephant," she said,
"huge like the fig tree on the eastern bank
of the Banaganga had snatched my son
and was flying across the sky like a rain cloud.
Stop I screamed,
don't go, don't take my son away,
but I found that I was unable to hear
the sound of my own words,
my lips were, as if, stitched together,
and my tongue was heavy
like the stone in the Shiva temple."

Now she was fast asleep
and who knows what dreams,
and of what colours,

were streaming
across the landscape of her imagination?
Rahul was tucked safely beside her,
her arm covering his little forehead.
Sukanta, the maid, was dozing,
her head resting on the right side of the bed.
The room was filled
with faint rhythmic snoring.

He looked at them
and found peeping through the sheet
her left foot,
ringed with a silver anklet,
soft, moist and warm
like the face of a new-born fawn.
"No I shouldn't," he commanded his hand to stay still,
turned around, ready to walk out,

when Yashodhara's arm
suddenly moved
uncovering Rahul's face.

O how beautiful,
small, round, fresh and inviting,
someone inside him spoke silently,
his legs trembled, and he knew
that he would have to sit down
for a while in the corner
and wait for the moment to pass.

Sukanta moved her head
rambled a few words in sleep
and the long hoot of an owl
outside the window shattered the peace.
He heard a flutter of wings,
and decided that it was time
for him to get up,
take a few steps and disappear in the moonlit night.

Chandaka was waiting
outside with the horse.
The three walked,
with their heads down
looking at their own shadows
and listening to the gravel
crunching under their feet.

Soon they would cross the river
walk through the woods
and in the first hour of the new-born day
Gautama would change into a saffron robe
obtained from a bemused hunter in exchange
for the princely one from Varanasi,
cut his long black hair,
ask Chandaka to drop it into the river,
and to tell his father, the King,
that life should continue as usual,
although he knew in his heart
that life would never be the same.

Autumn 1

A strange calm has suddenly descended.
The rains have all but gone and the Banaganga

doesn't seem so reckless. The sky is blue,
deep and clean like a blank slate on which

stray clouds now and then
manage to inscribe a few broken lines of wavy words.

Why is this calm
so deceptive, uncanny and unsettling?

Why can't I go out and like a wild
and mischievous deer let myself loose in the grassland

ready to explode with a musky fragrance?
Is this, I ask Vasudha, my friend, my soul mate,

because my heart is blocked, my eyes blinded,
and my ears waiting only to hear the sound of the familiar footsteps?

Autumn 2

Vasudha, who is madly in love
with the starry autumn sky, drags me out one night

to gaze at the divine celestial sea.
We lie on our backs and look at the stars staring back at us.

My eyes follow her finger,
glued to it as if it were a blindman's stick

and my mind a blank sheet of paper.
Cetus the whale, Delphinus the dolphin, Aquarius, Pisces,

the beautiful Capricornus, half goat
half fish, and Akashganga, the Milky Way,

dripping lazily into the sea.
Suddenly someone nudges me

and I am set adrift floating like a cloud
in the vast vibrant and voluptuous sky.

Autumn 3

Spring is far away,
but I miss the bitter-sweet taste of Jamun,

the Java Plum, of last spring.
You roll the plum in your mouth, suck its brown-purple skin,

press it gently between your teeth
and with a push of the tongue crack it open

to reach the red juicy flesh;
feel its stringy, sweet and spongy hardness, and let it disappear

till the tongue has the pleasure of caressing
the moist warm and striated roundness of the seed.

Don't spit the seed out
but wait till the mouth has accepted the next offering.

Isn't this strange, my love, that even
a small fleshy fruit can tingle such pleasure in the body?

Autumn 4

If you happen to walk past
the pond this autumn you'll find me talking to the fish.

What do you think about, I ask them,
when the soft rain of autumn hits the water?

Can you feel the drops
as they pierce the potted surface?

Do they in any way hurt you?
Or is their intrusion only mildly perturbing?

Do you sometimes look up, to peep at the sky,
and does the sky also seem to you distant and disinterested?

You need to believe me when I say
that I carry this sky with me like a dupatta.

But most of all, what I want to
know about is, the colour of your dreams.

Autumn 5

Vasudha often tells me
that I have turned into the harsingar

which you planted the day you married me.
Like the harsingar I bloom, she says, only when it is dark,

and with the first
ray of the sun, drops all its flowers.

In reply I smile, but don't tell her
that it's not the harsingar I seem to have changed into,

but the orange whorls that cocoon
the yet-to-grow, white, creamy flowers,

from which the sadhus make the dye
for their saffron robes. I know that it's only my imagination,

but I feel that the robe
which hugs your body is tinged with the juices of my flesh.

Autumn 6

What makes the corn
so soft, sweet and tepid like milk?

Is this the mild autumn rain
or the wind rustling gently through the fields?

No, it's the sun, Ma, Rahul tells me,
warm, soft and smooth like your belly.

When scared by a nightmare,
he comes to my bed at night and I find him sleeping

with his arm around me,
the thumb of his right hand beached safely in my navel.

It seems strange to me, my love,
that, like you, he should find my belly snug and cuddly.

Tell me, why do we find the roundness of shapes
so tempting that our hands can't resist caressing it?

Sujata's Kheer

He looks
so immaculate
this Gautama,
who has just become the Buddha.

I see him carved
in a huge wall of grainy
yellow sandstone
marked with ripples,
hands joined in his lap,
as if, holding the weight
of an invisible thought.

The head framed
by the corona of ten wheels
behind which
four Buddhas, two on each side,
stand in the sanctum of four temples.

The eyes,
shut behind petal-like lashes,
are focused on the open palms.

The nose is long and straight,
the lips, full and luscious,

holding silently the words
about to frame the thought.

The ears are perfect,
their elliptical curves
exaggerated by rings,
touching his broad shoulders.
The wavy texture of the sheet
draping his body,
drops from the left shoulder,
leaving the right side exposed
to reveal the beautiful button-like nipple.

On the face,
the hint of a hesitant smile
ready to calm and conquer
the uneasy turbulence
of an anxious thought.

Gautama had liked
the leafy woods
that spread on the western bank
of the river Niranjana,
not far from the happy village of Uruvilva.

Spring had brought
a sense of delight,
and he could feel
that his body was finding
the pleasure of travelling

to the centre of the thought
which would empty his body
and let him soar, like a falcon,
to the outer spheres of his being.

"Isn't it strange,"
he often asked himself,
"The more you try to rein in this body,
the more it reins you in?"

For months now,
he had practised absolute abstinence,
the denial of food, water and even breathing.
He would put a bowl full of water in front of him
and fight the urge to drink.
He would take a long breath
and keep the air in
till his head would be ready to explode.
He would deny every murmur of the body,
turn deaf to its most audible of whispers,
and try to de-congregate its fleshy solidness.

But it didn't work.

The body didn't stop whispering.
The more he denied it
the more it came back
in the form of pain
and loss of consciousness.

It kept on knocking at the door of his ego
to let it in, and to travel with his thoughts.

"Should I let go,
should I stop resisting?"

Thus, finally, he gave in.

The morning after a torrid night
spent suspended
in the twilight zone of
being and non-being
as he opened his eyes
he saw a young pretty girl
dressed in a yellow sari
dotted with red flowers
bend to put down a bowl of kheer,
rice boiled in creamy sweetened milk.

He got up,
walked up to the river
and slowly let himself
into the nice warm water.
He saw the fish
swish through his fingers and smiled.
A tiny green frog
sitting on a leaf jumped
and a bird flew across.

The world, he thought,
was, after all, not empty.

The rice was delicious.
He could feel it going down
through his body
filling it with a strange sensation,
as if he had turned into a sitar
and someone was playing on him,
plucking and stroking every string.
"Don't string the chords too tight,"
he remembered his teacher in Kapilavastu telling him,
"They will break,
but don't let them get slack either
because they will not make music."

That night, they say
he saw five dreams.

In the dreams,
his whole life,
the present
and the ones before it
flew past him.
He saw a golden peacock,
and said, that was I.
He saw a marsh crow
and said, that was I.
He saw a fig tree, a monkey, a lion,

an antelope, a rabbit and said
that was I that was also I.

After a while
he stopped saying it
because, whatever he saw
he saw himself in it.
If everything I see and saw is I
or was I, then what is I?
If I'm everywhere,
does it mean that I'm nowhere,
that if I become everything
I also become nothing,
an emptiness
brimming with the fullness of the world?

He had at last
found the way
to erase the face of his own ego.

He looked at the fig tree
as he lay in its benevolent shadow.
The sun was playing hide and seek
with the silky mass of leaves,
ants, spiders, all sorts of insects, twittering birds,
and two monkeys ready to jump and swing.

The tree
and the world around the tree

had come together.
"I need to turn into a tree," he told himself.

He spent forty-nine days, they say,
under the same tree.
Then got up,
put his wooden slippers on,
and walked in the direction of Varanasi
where he would deliver his first sermon.

Winter 1

It is the sky that I love the most in winter.
An endless dome of a celestial temple speckled with stars.

The waxing crescent
and her bright stud in the nose, the yellow Shukra tara.*

What promise does it bring?
What hope, or is it just a ray of light leading nowhere?

I wonder if you look at the same sky
and with the same eyes, and does it also fill you with sad joy

that throbs through my body
and makes me feel that although I am dead

some part of me is still living,
waiting for a sign, a gesture, perhaps the streak of a shooting star

to let me know that although
you are trying your best, it's not so easy for you to forget me.

* Venus.

Winter 2

The grass is covered with dew
and as I walk in the garden the cold shoots up

through my soles,
trying to shake me out of blissful slumber.

Throughout the night the dew rained
and the ashoka tree outside the window creaked.

That night, in my dream
I saw two brown owls on the tree hoot and screech

then fly off. Where have
they gone? I walk thinking and suddenly find

on the wet grass under the tree
a clump of tawny spotted feathers.

As I bend to pick them up,
the tree shakes its head as if in disbelief, wetting me all over.

Winter 3

O how blissful is this sun
that wraps your body like a warm silky quilt.

I have always wondered
what is it that makes your body feel like a body?

The touch of a hand, a kiss,
a shooting pain or a pair of eyes looking at you intently.

But it's Rahul's feet that
I remember most, when holding my fingers he walked on my belly,

his eyes looking straight at me,
mouth open, teeth white as milk, and face nothing but laughter.

Now he walks holding the hand of his dadu,
your father, solemn, sincere and full of purpose.

He is only four, I tell myself and curse
for letting him grow out of his childhood so soon.

Winter 4

I wish I could gather my black shawl,
hide my face and step out in this cold misty night

to join the singers sitting around the fire
under the thin shadow of the fourth-night moon.

The old man would look at me, smile,
and raising his blind eyes towards the sky let the song go.

The young girl would pass me her dhol
and help me strike the right beat to join

the swinging sounds of manjira, kartal and dotara.
The night would drift on the waves of music. The faces

would shimmer in the flickering tongues of fire,
and the taste of sweet potatoes would wrap around the words.

But, my love, this would never happen.
The place of a queen, I know, is inside the palace.

Winter 5

Do you remember the kachnar
that grew near the pond in our garden?

The one that used to shed
its leaves in winter but always hesitated to blossom.

Suddenly this winter
as if touched by the gracious hand of the blessed one

it has finally
resolved to splash all its colours.

What a wondrous opulence of mauve,
magenta and pink! Even the fish in the pond

have lost their way
under the heady fragrance that swoops on you as you walk past.

O shameless, I scold her, why this season,
when it seems the world inside me has turned so blank and dull?

Winter 6

I am sick and the fever has
invaded every inch of my flesh and bones.

For three days and nights I have slept inside,
covered by quilts, blankets and spreads.

I can hear the sweet devil
walk through me like an eager and indulging lover,

turning me into a flaming furnace.
Soon the sweat explodes through every pore of my body

and a coolness descends
that reminds me of a breeze flowing through mountain valleys.

After a few hours the fever strikes again
and like a pitcher I am lowered again into the dark abyss of a well.

The only joy is Rahul who places his hand on my forehead,
kisses me, and says, "You'll get better Ma, you'll get better soon."

The Buddha Grafts a White Mango Tree

If you are a god
or a saint we expect
a miracle or two from you,
and if you are not a god or a saint
but a run-of-the-mill human
and have somehow been able
to conjure a miracle,
something unusual, unnatural,
something that fails to fall in line with that
which we have come to call the real,
we begin to see
a godly or perhaps
saintly presence in you.

Thus when the Buddha
was acknowledged as the Buddha,
the enlightened one, who not only knew
how to read the complicated patterns of life and death
but had also guessed the ways and means to extract oneself
from this endless cycle of coming and going,
the people around him,
including a crowd of the saffron robed bhikshus
had begun praying for a miracle or two to unfold.

He saw that written
all over their faces.
They, the bhikshus, prayed to know
if what they had come to believe
was really believable,
that their faith was not misplaced,
that their Buddha was really
the Buddha.

Often he looked away
scared of the intensity
with which their eyes probed,
asked, pleaded and waited for the inevitable.

He was, I believe,
a prisoner of his own
enlightened consciousness.

Otherwise,
he lived a disciplined,
almost, mechanical life,
getting up well before dawn,
washing in the nearby pond or river
and meditating either sitting cross-legged
or pacing in a measured way
back and forth
under a shady tree.

When it was light
he would take his bowl

and walk to the nearest village,
alone or with a flock of bhikshus.
He would knock at the first door,
wait for it to open,
and accept whatever was dropped in the bowl.

Begging,
he often told the monks,
was good for you.
It made you look at the world from below,
to know how it feels to be low,
stuck at the bottom of the pile called humanity.

He would stay
at the door silent like a statue
and, if it failed to open,
walk to the next and knock again.

Once the bowl was full
he would return to his resting place,
eat his meal for the day,
and busy himself
in the task of building the sangha.

"Take life as it comes
and do whatever you have to do
as if you were outside it.
Don't muddy the waters with your presence.
Let the river flow around you touching and cleansing.
It will always find the shape

and sense of your being.
Swim like a fish oblivious of the water,
fly like a bird
without noticing
the colour of the sky
and the force of the wind.
Avoid passion and belonging.
Know that knowing itself
is nothing but giving in,
and the desire to possess
brings you closer
to the state of being yourself possessed."

I guess, at times,
he himself was scared
of this utter detachment.
Can you be a lotus
and yet remain aloof from the silky water
that ebbs and flows around you?
Can you look away from the fish
that swirl and dance and flirt with your roots?
Can you really resist the fatal attraction of
your image flickering in the water?

Thus, one day,
as if to test his resolve,
the news,
which he first thought was nothing but a rumour,
was brought to him,
that in the great northern battle,

the whole clan of the Sakyas,
the people with whom
he shared blood, water, land and air,
was being slaughtered
by the cruel king of the Kosalas.

He heard silently the stories
and raised his right hand to bless
the few survivors
who had come to ask for his advice,
but he didn't dare even to think
of the miracle with which
he could have saved his people.

It's true
that he had over the years,
here and there,
performed miracles,
usual for gods and saints of his stature:

He had once split wooden logs
just by looking at them,
had made the waters of a river part
and showed his power to walk on air.

Once he even made
the clouds burst
and the rain to fall only
over the heads of the chosen ones.

These miracles were harmless, innocent,
and the intention was merely to help him
win some small religious tussles
or to convert those who were hard to impress.

He loved to stay in parks
and mango groves
that stood not far from towns and villages.

From there
he could be with his people
without being too close to them.
They came to him in droves
to listen to his sermons
and be blessed by his mere presence.

The miracle,
if it was a miracle,
was performed in a mango grove
close to the town of Sravasti.
It was the sixth year
following the enlightenment,
and he was fighting the challenge
posed by the six teachers of a rival sect.

The debate was intense
and the bhikshus were anxious,
that's when, one day, he stood up
and first water like a river flowed through his feet,
followed by fire,

and before the crowd could come to terms
with what they had seen,
he invoked another
more marvellous scene for them to remember:

He first disappeared
and when they looked for him
they found four Buddhas
in four different positions
occupying the canopy
of a huge mango tree in full bloom.

That year
the tree didn't bear any fruit,
as if shell-shocked
and still recovering from the trance.
When the wind blew
it shook its head like a mad
intoxicated elephant,
scaring the monkeys away.

It took three years
for the tree to regain its fleshy fruity self.
The mangos were large, juicy,
with a small pea-size stone,
and were sweet like honey.
The difference was
that the skin of the mangos was white,
whiter than the white lotuses and lilies
that stood in the pond.

At night
in the light of the full moon
the green tree with white mangos
was a marvellous sight,
but no one dared to touch the fruit.
They hung majestically
tempting the eyes
with their voluptuous roundness and gleaming skin.

Their look was so engaging
that people forgot
that they were meant to be eaten.
Even the birds and the monkeys
found them too exotic.

The white mango tree
was thus marooned for ever,
waiting to be rescued by a story or a poem.

The Cool 1

Palas, the flame of the forest,
is in full bloom. How ugly it was just a few months ago.

An unruly mass of crooked
and twisted leafless branches covered by a rough grey bark.

But now it has gone mad,
flashing its wealth of orange, yellow and vermilion flowers,

studded in velvety green cups.
You used to call it the parrot tree, pointing at the

beak-shaped keels of flowers.
But it seems it's not the parrots that come to the tree

but swarms of sunbirds with yellow backs,
gold-crested mynas, and brown spotted babblers.

What do I see? I ask myself, a tree immersed
in a wild cacophony — a tree-bird as well as a bird-tree?

The Cool 2

The word you are waiting for
is shaping itself in the unseen folds of your body.

You can feel it wreath and roll in the belly
and like a snow-ball grow into a sonorous coagulum,

thick, light, airy and moist like the early morning fog.
It fills your lungs, creeps along the walls of the windpipe,

making you breathless for a while
and then stays glued onto the tongue like the taste of a kiss.

You are not sure if you want it to stay
or to come out into the world sopping with sounds and babble.

But when at last it makes its way forward, the flood gates open.
Words followed by words, slot into neat or clumsy sentences.

The poem begins to find its feet.
I know I am not a poet, but who can affront the onslaught of spring?

The Cools

I can't forget the coy
but friendly smile of the potter sitting behind his wheel.

With a stick held in both hands,
he spun the wheel, sat down, and the yellowish lumps of clay

coaxed and flattered by his hands
began to find their forms, when suddenly he looked up

to intercept my gaze grazing his face.
Did he catch the sight of the veiled potter that lives in my body?

He brought clay from the banks of the Banaganga,
water from the pond smelling of lotuses and lilies,

and shaped two vases
now drying in the warm sunshine of the young spring,

and as I look at them,
I know that there is somewhere, a river flowing in me.

The Cool 4

The two vases which the potter
left last month in the courtyard to dry, are waiting for flowers.

No, they are not waiting for flowers.
They don't know what it means to wait for someone.

It is I who have walked the entire length
and breadth of emptiness, and read silent words on blank pages.

No, I won't bring them flowers.
Let them, like me, enjoy the flight of the bird called expectation.

I have often seen the bird
hop in through the window, sit at the corner of the bed and fly off,

leaving not only feathers
but also the invisible contours of its flight in the air.

Tell me, my love,
is remembering nothing but a torrid journey to forgetting?

The Cool 5

Yellow is the colour of the young
and exuberant spring making its way across the banks

of the Banaganga. The fields awash
with pungent mustard, swooning at the slightest

incitement of a breeze. Two rivers
like two herds of adolescent elephants walking leisurely,

their muddied backs bobbing up and down,
when suddenly a pair of large white egrets breaks into flight.

The sky quivers, the eye follows
the flutter of wings for a while and returns to the mango groves

crowned with a multitude of white,
green and yellow flowers. The air is full of such promise

and hope that my heart despairs,
unwilling to believe that the promise will come true.

The Cool 6

The early morning sky
is so deep and blue that it hurts the eyes.

It's best to keep them shut
and let the sky drape the fragments of dreams

which fill your body. Their residue
like an afterglow warms and tints your vision

as you listen to the woodpecker
knocking on the dry branches of the mango.

The monotone beat is interrupted by silences
lined with the breeze shuffling through the leaves.

A cloud of lightness grows around you
and like a forlorn feather you are lifted into the wilderness.

No, I'm not sick my love, it's just that a cloud
entered me last night when I was dreaming about you.

Ananda: the Bahusruta

I don't know what to
write about you, Ananda,
what words, of what length,
sound and rhythm need I call upon
to do justice to your story.

Or should I forget
the thought of justice
because stories, as you know,
are always tainted, tilted and tattooed?

No, I should put aside
the foolish idea
that you need to be rescued,
restored and rewritten.
I should, instead,
do what I have to do,
and tell the story as I feel fit.
I need to remember
that I am nothing but a minor poet,
a scribbler, a writer of no consequence.

But you, Ananda,
were not a minor protagonist
although you had lived

most of your life
like an eclipsed moon,
and even when you got the chance
to shine full on your own,
you and everyone around you
knew that the gleaming light
was that of the Buddha.

Tell me, how does it feel
to live like a mushroom
in the shadow of a tall leafy oak?
Do you get to glimpse the stars
in the clear winter sky?
Do you feel the shadows of rain clouds
drift over your head?
And what about the wind
which shakes the oak
like a giant rhinoceros?
You must, I believe,
have felt only a few stray whiffs and wafts
of the unruly turbulence.

For twenty-five years
you had lived with the Buddha,
like his shadow,
fetched food and water for him,
dyed and mended his robes,
prepared his bed,
and when he was sick
washed, cleaned, dressed and undressed him.

I can understand your desperation
when the day after the funeral of the Buddha,
the bhikshus put you on a show-trial.

Four hundred and ninety-nine of them
stood in a semicircle
with Bhikshu Mahakashyapa,
the "great turtle", in the centre,
asking you strange, odious and incriminating questions,
for which you struggled to find adequate answers.

Your silence fanned their anger,
they shook their heads,
raised their hands,
and inaudible whispers
soon grew into a loud uproar.

In the sea of saffron robes,
you, dressed in your white kurta and dhoti,
were a tiny white speck.
They disliked your otherness,
your being amongst them,
and yet not with them,
free, autonomous and relaxed.
No doubt
they decided
to throw you out of the sangha.

But they were plagued with doubts.
You were, they knew, the Bahusruta,

the one who had heard every word,
the one in whom
the dharma had found residence,
and the only one
through whom it could be re-stored, ordered and set adrift
to spread, swell and proliferate.

They needed you.

Thus one rainy night
when you suddenly
knocked at the door,
the "great turtle" let you in
and found a suitable place for you.

A few weeks
after your arrival,
he summoned the bhikshus again.
They sat in a circle
on the flat top of a grassy mound
and repeated after you
the sutras that you had heard,
or which you or they believed you had heard.
The dharma was
thus ordered neatly into separate baskets
to suit the needs of the bhikshus,
the ardent followers, and the lay people.

The way had been opened for you,
the residue of the Buddha,

to be ordained
and become the new helmsman.

Soon you would find yourself
written into each and every story
that I now read about the Buddha:
you are the jackal, the tree sprite,
the otter, the king, the mahout….

I think, I am selfish,
perhaps silly, when I say
that I am disappointed with your coronation,
and that I would have liked you
to have died in your white-unordained robe,
and vanished like a ripple
or a word whispered gently into the air.

Yes, I don't understand
the tyranny of history,
and the way it is written and overwritten.

Spring I

There is a spring painted in my eyes
that blinds me from the one that is outside.

There is a spring painted in my head
that tells me not to see as it's to be seen.

There is a spring painted in my heart
that forbids me from forgetting how it was.

There is a spring painted in my body
that asks me to forego any semblance of desire.

No, there is, in fact, no spring,
but for the remains of a bygone spring

which I have gathered and stored away.
There won't be any more springs for me to live.

Life has found its pattern
in which neither present nor future is of any consequence.

Spring 2

The spring has now let itself loose
like a cunning and brazen courtesan

trying its best to sell its charm and splendour.
O shameless, I scold her, why don't you hide

your opulent plenitude
and let me get on with my un-eventful act of living.

I do have to walk a million miles
before I cross the dark and dreary landscape of my being.

Don't distract me with your colours,
smells and sounds, and leave me alone

to weave the web of words
with which I wish to catch a few scraps of memory.

Isn't it true, my love, that we need words
to keep the stories afloat in the stormy sea of time?

Spring3

No, I have never seen the blue expanse
of the sea, an overturned dome of a moonless sky.

But I have heard its roar
and its gentle — like a lullaby — splash from a poet

who came to us a couple of years ago.
His face was swathed with wrinkles, his head shaved,

hands crusty and fingers long and knotty.
He played his bamboo flute and the lashes over his

blind eyes fluttered. "I can't see your face Ranima,"
he had said, "but in your voice I feel the restrained vowels of sadness.

You need to go to the sea,
smell its salty breath and wash your body with sand."

It was spring then, glorious and sumptuous,
and I knew it was the spring that was at the heart of my sadness.

Spring 4

Once again the girls
have hurled the swings around the supple

and sturdy branches of the mighty figs,
donned their bright red, yellow and green dupattas

lined with gold and silver threads,
and let their bodies swing like birds in flight.

They sing as they push
the swings up with their legs, their ankles shimmering

like fish in water, the drums urging them
not to give up till their feet touch the branches

and their laughter ripples through the leaves.
On the ground the monkeys look bewildered

and even the placid buffaloes stop munching,
wondering what has happened to the mute giant tree.

Spring 5

It's the month of Vaisakha,
and your mother has forbidden me

to wear white colourless clothes.
She wants me to smile and look buoyant, happy,

and to understand that you, my love,
are not dead but have just walked away

in search of love and peace
and would return one day triumphant like a god.

Then you would be there, she assures me,
to be shared with everyone like the air we breathe.

Most of all she wants me to remember
that some thirty springs ago, when the full moon was

shedding milk and honey,
you made your way into this joyful and miserable world.

Spring 6

I saw you the other night
walk into my room with a lamp in your right hand.

In the flickering light,
smelling of camphor and jasmine, your face

without a smile, like a carved piece of stone
with ghostly eyes, fixed somewhere beyond me

outside the walls. A face so familiar
but so removed, indifferent, uncanny.

Tell me, why did I wish
that you would put the lamp away, remove your robe,

and get in beside me in the bed?
Didn't I know that you'd take a few steps

and disappear through the walls
into the spring, oblivious of time, place and seasons?

Gautama is Born

We look at a tree,
its wholeness
shaped by the trunk,
leaves, branches, flowers and fruits;
the wind shuffling through its supple body,
the sky seeping through its crevices,
and the birds nesting in its cuddly expanse, and imagine
that it was all locked up in the seed
waiting to unfurl, unfold, unravel.

It's in the seed
we deposit our hopes.
It's the seed
we embellish with fantasy and frisson.

Did the same
happen to the Buddha and his story?
Wasn't it written after his death?

He had already walked on this earth
as the enlightened one,
bringing miracles, healings and deliverance.

You, like me,
were a zealous teller of stories

and a petty scribbler
for whom it was a challenge
and a chance not to be missed.
Now you could invoke all your charm,
artistry, and resources
to weave a web of words
to catch the Buddha like a fish.

You didn't know then,
that as the story
would begin to find its shape
you yourself would be caught in the net.

It was an ordeal,
a task quite difficult to manage.
There was an excess in the Buddha,
an abundance that was scary,
a boundless profundity.

Like the sculptor
who carved the panel in the
dark temple cave in south India,
you didn't know
how to grasp the un-graspable.

One can't see
the Buddha in the carving.
The space under the parasol
between two fly whisks
is the place

where the new-born Buddha
is invisibly visible,
an emptiness pregnant with presence.

Thus, you also thought
to describe the Buddha
with silences,
to leave blanks in your story
for the readers to fill in.

But you failed miserably.

Too much freedom,
as we know, is no freedom.

Thus instead of blanks
you decided to negotiate the excess
with an excess of embellishments,
to decorate words with festoons of images,
metaphors and metonyms.

Now I know
why an immaculate conception
was essential for Gautama,
the would-be Buddha.
He was conceived in a dream
and a dream he was for humanity
suffering from disease, death and disintegration.

One summer night
when Queen Mayadevi was sleeping
on the roof of her palace
covered by the canopy of stars,
a tiny elephant entered her right side.
A rain of shooting stars
splintered the sky
and the heavens hummed.

Ten lunar months later
Gautama was born.
The queen was going home to her parents
when on the way
near the sala grove at Lumbini,
she suddenly felt
that the baby-elephant
was ready to break through.

It's said
that she stood near a pond
holding the branch of a tree
and the boy made his way out
through the right side.

He neither cried nor smiled
but climbed up a large lotus flower
that had suddenly sprouted near the pond.
He was bathed by gods and kings
and walked seven steps
towards each of the principal directions.

From the way he walked,
it was clear that one day
he would circumscribe
the whole world,
and that the world would come to rest in his palm
like a round pebble
warmed by the summer sun.

In his first walk
a white parasol
sheltered his head,
similar to the one
which we see in the stone carving.

For the rest of his life
the parasol would go
wherever he went.

The queen passed away
seven days after giving birth.
The role assigned to her was fulfilled.

She had become redundant
to the story
and the life behind it.

Poetry Series

1. Ouyang Yu, *Songs of the Last Chinese Poet.*
   ISBN: 0 9586526 4 3; 1997; 95 pp. Softcover.

2. Ouyang Yu, *Two Hearts, Two Tongues and Rain-coloured Eyes.*
   ISBN: 1 8769570 2 6; September 2002; 118 pp. Softcover.

3. Zijie Pan, *Vostok & This Could Have Happened to You.*
   ISBN: 1 8769570 3 4; September 2002; 94 pp. Softcover.

4. Subhash Jaireth, *Yashodhara: Six Seasons Without You.*
   ISBN: 1 876957 05 0; September 2003, 78 pp. Softcover.